LAUGHING in the REIGN

SURVIVING THE CRAZY, HILARIOUS, SCARY TIMES OF BUSH, OBAMA, TRUMP, AND BIDEN

RUSS FEDORKA

working-class cartoonist

Editing and Technical Layout
Tim Gaughan

Preface by labor historian
Paul LeBlanc

LAUGHING IN THE REIGN

ISBN: 978-1-66788-014-3

CONTENTS

IN THE TRADITION OF
RADICAL WORKER-CARTOONISTS

Paul Le Blanc

I f you look at the art and cartoons that sparked up the pages of radical working-class newspapers and magazines of the early 1900s in the United States—especially prevalent in the publications of the Industrial Workers of the World (IWW)—you will see multiple creations of clever and creative worker-cartoonists, who were able to capture the complexities of their time with dramatic and often humorous images. Russ Fedorka is a modern-day representative of that tradition—exposing the complexities of our own time by looking beneath the surface, often with a good laugh, to trace the simple realities underlying all of that.

Over the years, a number of us in the Pittsburgh area came to know Russ as an unpretentious and dedicated activist in a variety of struggles for peace and social justice—a radical-minded, down-to-earth, very decent guy who could always be relied on to help out in the struggle for a better world. We also knew that he was an experienced construction worker and could help those who needed help in fixing up their homes.

A very modest and relatively stable kind of a guy, he could hardly be described as being "full of surprises"—but there were a couple of ways in which he truly startled me. One surprise was delivered when he was listening intently, off on to the side, as I was immersed in a conversation with a young activist. I was patiently explaining why we must build a movement capable of reaching out to the working-class majority, ultimately helping to mobilizing it to establish social ownership and democratic control over our economic resources. Without this, we would never overcome the terrible impacts of the powerful minority of profiteers making a mess of our world. After she thanked me for sharing these ideas, assuring me that she would give it all serious thought, Russ approached me. He told me he wanted to join the socialist organization to which I was seeking to recruit our younger friend. And he became a genuine stalwart of that organization (which our friend also ended up joining). With Russ, it was clear that he was motivated not simply by words from discussions and reading, but by the experience of his life.

WHY SHOULD WORKERS PRODUCE FOR IDLERS?   (IWW)

The other surprise was that Russ is a cartoonist whose sharp-witted images can convey what might take an educational and agitational speaker a full-scale lecture to communicate. His artistry helped to enliven the perhaps overly wordy pages of *The New People*.

Russ's ability to see through the clutter of rhetoric, cutting to the heart of the matter, is demonstrated over and over in these cartoons which introduce viewers to the U.S. political scene in the opening decades of the twenty-first century. One might have a legitimate quibble with one or another nuance in what Russ presents, but it seems to me that a well-informed person would have a difficult time in honestly disagreeing with the thrust of his vision.

Now He Understands The Game

Solidarity, November 11, 1916.

In what Russ offers, there is continuity but also innovation. The worker-cartoonists of the early twentieth century had important points to make in their time, but Russ—shaped by unfolding realities of later years—has new and different images to share. His understanding of the working-class majority highlights a diversity and range of issues that sometimes eluded earlier artists. The new varieties of technology and media glitz abound in what he presents us. The expertise of the bought-and-paid-for "hidden persuaders" have introduced innumerable new ways to fool us. But Russ is on to them, and the still-valid insights of the old worker-cartoonists are therefore brought to life in what he shares with us.

A NOTE FROM THE ARTIST

The cartoons of an era tell a particular kind of story of that era. They capture the pulse and brush on the dreams of their time.

In compiling these cartoons, I began realizing that it would be important to do justice to the bigger picture, or the story of those times. This is true even of the early roots of my artwork, but even more with what is presented in this book. While I was with the Thomas Merton Center's *New People* monthly newspaper, there was a people's story going on—starting with Obama's startling backsliding and betrayals, through the stunning, bizarre Trump era—full of colorful characters throughout, that set the tone and substance of the era. There were the highs of such things as the Occupy Movement, the Black Lives Matter movement, and the Million Woman March offsetting the lows of Obama's progressive betrayals and Trump's insanity. It's all part of the story.

But I realize that my own story has been part of the larger story. So, here is at least part of my story; you might say I was born into both politics and art. My mother was an accomplished commercial artist at G.C. Murphy's company in McKeesport, Pennsylvania. She was a Kennedy Democrat. Her family had to be split up during the Great Depression — very traumatic. During the 1930s, many people in McKeesport were drawn into industrial union struggles, and to the New Deal of Franklin D. Roosevelt. My uncles on my mother's side were all strong FDR Union Democrats. Her father was an early member of the union movement, known as the Congress of Industrial Organizations (CIO).

My grandfather would tell me stories of the Pinkerton men, union busters, including being shot at from rooftops. He told me that when he was ten years old, he worked with other kids, 10-hour days, six days a week. One boss would even yell, beat, and kick the kids. My grandfather told me years later, when he was in his twenties, he ran into that boss at a local after-work bar. The boss wanted my grandfather to just forget about it, but my grandfather, quite literally, knocked him out instead. My grandfather was an outspoken Union man all the way—all the time. He was small but tough as nails, raised in a family of boxers, baseball players, and pool sharks.

My father was a big part of my life—deeply loved by my whole family. He had lots of friends because he was so warm and fun to be with. Although he had no formal technical training, he would put his hand to various aspects of auto repair and construction—and even fixing air conditioners. A great communicator, he was a successful salesman for Pomco (the now defunct Potter-McCune Company), food distributors in the Tri-State area of Pennsylvania, Ohio, and West Virginia. He wasn't particularly political, but he taught me "people skills," especially how to treat all people with respect.

I grew up in the last days of the Union majority stronghold in the working class and was stirred into anti-war activism with the help of my good buddy Bill Neander (who passed away in 2010). Bill talked me into skipping school in 1967 to join an anti-war protest in McKeesport that featured the Berrigan brothers. I still remember some of the points they made about lobbyists for companies like Exxon and Goodyear, lobbying Congress for more war, and that the Gulf of Tonkin incident (when the North Vietnamese allegedly attacked U.S. Naval vessels) was a lie. A dedicated anti-war resistor was born that day, and I never regretted it or looked back.

After graduating high school, I quickly found out "long-haired hippie types need not apply." So, I got a job at a sweatshop; that turned out to be a learning experience too. We were being squeezed too hard at the sweatshop, so we workers put our foot down as a collective force. Our wildcat strike changed the atmosphere for the better, and high-fives among the workers reflected their joy. Lesson learned: the people united can change the world.

I went to college for a while after that and got into counterculture-based trouble there. I will say one thing for my college days: I had some very good professors that inspired me to try to get history right, along with other things. After that, I tried small farming with a group of friends for a year or so (you could call it a commune), then moved to Boston with the Young Socialist Alliance, to join the revolution—a few years early perhaps. This was also the period when I was drawing my early stuff, inspired by Abby Hoffman.

In the years that followed, I was able to gain experience as a construction worker and became a sub-contractor in general construction. In my heyday, I had about twelve guys working for me and with me. After about a year, an economic downturn wiped us out, but I was able to find remodeling work with small crews, collaborating with other contractors, and on my own.

It was also in this period that I got married and helped bring a wonderful daughter and son into the world. I am happy that I was able to be a coach for each of their soccer teams, and I am proud that they have both gone on to make meaningful lives for themselves. It feels like a special bonanza that my daughter has brought into being my beautiful granddaughter.

Years passed before the artist in me would pick up the pen and paper again; it was quite by accident. I volunteered to do ceiling repair and patch work at Pittsburgh's Thomas Merton Center. Since the 1970s, the Merton Center (founded by Molly Rush of Plowshares 8 fame), has been working for peace and social justice. I noticed some of the editors of the *New People* newspaper were there, so I mentioned I had some artwork the newspaper might be interested in. They looked at the work and agreed—the rest is history, 11-plus years of political cartoons. I was also politically active throughout this period, in the Thomas Merton Center's anti-war committee, and the Pittsburgh branch of the International Socialist Organization (ISO). The commitment to anti-war struggle and socialism has been a lifelong priority for me.

I hope you find these cartoons funny, inspiring, and food for thought. As you think of the times they reveal, in a cartoons' unique kind of way. Happy travels!

Russ Fedorka
Pittsburgh
October 2022

ACKNOWLEDGEMENTS

I would like to thank the people who have helped in making this book a reality.

Starting with The Three Amigos of Paul LeBlanc, Tim Gaughan (and myself). The three of us collaborated on numerous projects over the last decade, mostly with the Pittsburgh ISO and the Thomas Merton Center. Without their knowledge and guidance (along with Tim's editing and my son-in-law Elliott's technical help), this book would not have happened.

Other folks instrumental in developing this book: my mother's career in art, my grandfather's love of the working class, my father's amicability and organizational skills, and all the friends past and present from the TMC. Especially the wonderful peace activists of the recent past, including Dorothy Day and Edith Bell.

This book is dedicated to my buddy Bill Neander, and to all that have fought for peace and an end to war.

Thank you all!

Russ Fedorka

CAPITAL'S END

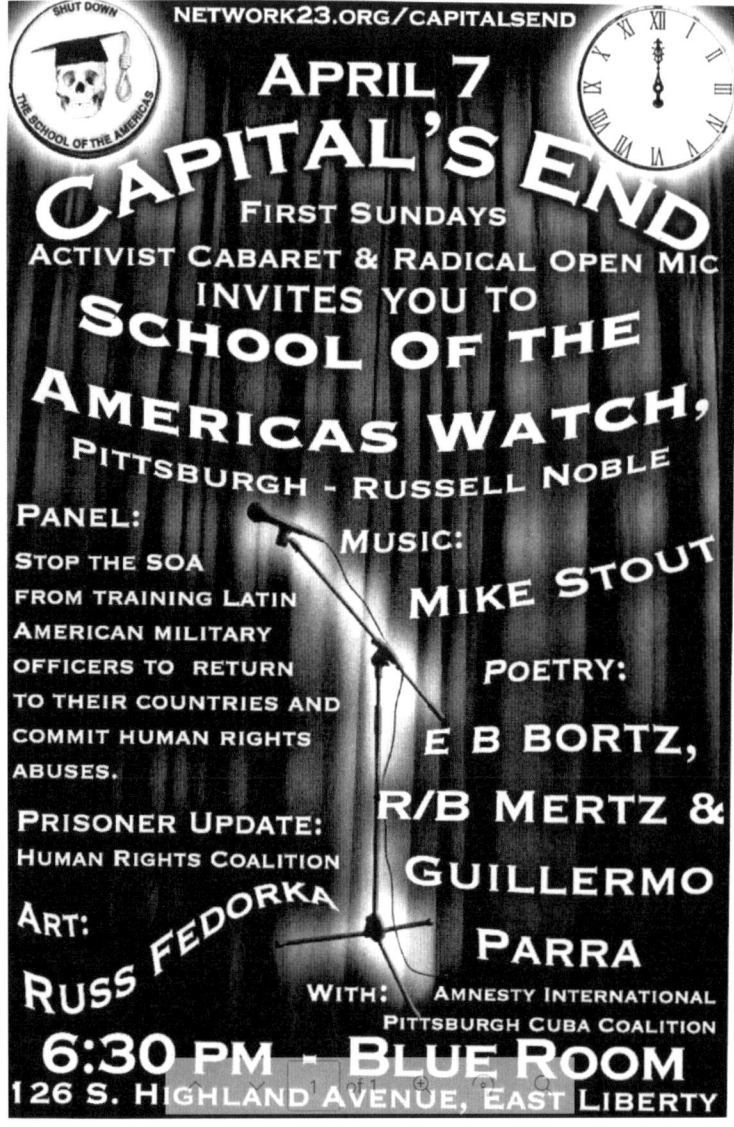

A few years ago, my friend Harvey Holtz started a weekly event called "Capital's End" at a friendly restaurant in Pittsburgh. It was a space where people got together to exchange ideas and enjoy music and entertainment. There were speeches and debates offered by all kinds of radicals and interesting people. We also had an open mic so everyone could speak their piece. I worked with Harvey on those events and designed this poster.

WORKERS OF THE WORLD UNITE!

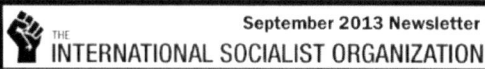
September 2013 Newsletter
INTERNATIONAL SOCIALIST ORGANIZATION

REBEL CITIES
Building Urban Insurgencies to Democratically Transform Society

David Harvey's book, *Rebel Cities*, asks how cities might be reorganized in more socially just and ecologically sane ways—and how they can become the focus for anti-capitalist resistance. Our continuing discussions, facilitated by Carl Redwood and other community activists and advocates will seek to apply Harvey's concepts to the practical realities of Pittsburgh, focusing on building grassroots struggles for positive change.

TUESDAY, Oct. 29, 7:30-9:00 p.m. THOMAS MERTON CENTER 5129 Penn Avenue
For more information, please contact Paul.LeBlanc@laroche.edu or helengerhardt1@gmail.com

Violently Numb

As I listened to Dave Zirin's *Edge of Sports* radio show discuss the violence of the National Football League a couple weeks ago, I began to think how our world is inherently violent in every aspect of our lives. A sport, like American football, represents a part in this violent society. The show, at one point discussed how NFL highlight reels are made with the focus of the reel being big plays, big hits and the player flexing their muscles after the big "pop." Violence seeps from American football, as it does in all society.

Violence is everywhere we turn. Then I began to think of all the violent stories and events happening over the last few weeks. Syria. Iraq. Afghanistan. Egypt. Greece. Washington D.C. All of these places suffered great violence, but one type of violence stuck out the most: state-sanctioned violence.

Two years ago on September 21, 2011, Troy Davis, an innocent man, suffered lethal violence at the hands of the state of Georgia. Davis was convicted and sentenced to death row in 1991 for killing a Savannah police officer. Since then, nine eyewitnesses retracted their statements and say Davis was an innocent man. However, this would not stop Davis' execution. Davis' story barely made headlines in the corporate news, but this tragedy shines a light on our violent society. This state sanctioned murder is one of many in our prison industrial complex. Go further it is a small part of a bigger pie which includes drone strikes, night raids, economic sanctions, "humanitarian aid," neglect of the poor, racism and sexism, the war on "insert your war of choice here" and the list continues.

Have we become numb to violence? Numb enough to let an innocent man, like most victims of the forms of violence listed above, die? If we all take a step back, we will realize violence is a big problem in our society and it stretches from our culture to our politics. Through collective action, we can overcome such a monster. Activists groups against the death penalty have the same fight as the anti-war movement. Activists groups against police brutality struggle against the same atrocities as women's rights groups. Activists groups against racism suffer along with those in the environmental movement. We are all connected through our collective struggle against violence, violence able to de-

The Pittsburgh branch of the International Socialist Organization (ISO) put out a monthly newsletter for a while. It covered a variety of topics and artwork.

CRAZY DAYS

I drew this in the early 1970s while living in Boston. It's just a reflection of what I was feeling at the time.

ABBIE IN AMERICA

Also from the early 70s, honoring Abbie Hoffman (as he had to go underground to avoid prosecution and capture by the FBI), reflecting his impressions of America.

"JUST WAR" IN AFGHANISTAN

The Obama administration's misguided policies in the Afghanistan war, and General Stanley McChrystal's insistence on doubling-down on the failed policies of a "limited war" in a third-world country. The war was only 9 years old at the time.

REPUBLICRAT DINER

The Democrats and Republicans control the political process and serve their Wall Street Overlords.

NATURE FIGHTS BACK

The revolt of plants, animals, and insects against a toxic company that is threatening their lives.

SCHOOL FOR REPUBLICANS

Karl Rove instructing Sarah Palin and George Bush to use the thinly veiled lexicon of empire.

THE REPUBLICAN FIELD

Preparing for the 2012 elections were Mitt Romney, PA's own Rick Santorum, and Newt Gingrich. All candidates must be approved by the 1% (screw the 99%).

ALL LIFE FORM ALERT!

As corporations prepared to initiate fracking to extract gas from the Marcellus Shale, PA's Fish and Boat Commissioner shrugged off the impending water pollution claiming it was safe. It's not safe at all.

OIL CORP ENTERTAINMENT

All Hail Big Oil! Cultural, economic, and environmental slime—but notice the protestors outside the windows.

OCCUPY PITTSBURGH!

The Occupy Wall Street movement swept across the country, including Pittsburgh. This changed the lingo of the day—we are the 99%!

SCHOOL OF THE AMERICAS
(WHINSEC)

The SOA, established by the U.S. government to aid "security forces" in Latin America, was recently renamed The Western Hemisphere Institute for Security Cooperation (WHINSEC). It teaches political repression, torture, controlling the press, overthrowing left-wing governments, and rooting out Indigenous people—all the dark sciences.

Turbocharged under the Reagan Administration, it is a horrible blemish on American history. It's also been one of my favorite places to protest.

BAD NEWS

Just a couple of space aliens' observations of planet Earth; no intelligent life.

LOWER QUALITY OF LIFE

Democratic and Republican leaders Obama and Mitt Romney relax over a meal while the working class is pushed into suffering. No war but Class War!

MAKING THE WORLD SAFE

Joint Special Operations Command (JSOC) is part of the United States Special Operations Command. It's charged with developing and executing "special operations" worldwide—including running covert, criminal, illegal wars. This highlights the power of the Military-Industrial Complex (MIC) over all Presidents.

PRIVATIZE

Pennsylvania's Republican Governor Tom Corbett pushed for privatization and downplayed the dangers of fracking.

Also referenced is Supreme Court Justice Clarence Thomas's dismissiveness of so-called "racial entitlements."

DRONE ON

There was unprecedented build-up of the Drone Warfare program by the Obama Administration, among other disappointments, while the Republicans continued to emphasize their severe aversion to any taxes on the wealthy.

The Alan Kieda reference was a bizarre overreach by the FBI because his name sounded like Al-Qaeda. (No shit!)

DON'T ASK AWKWARD QUESTIONS

The American Legislative Exchange (ALEC), is an organization of conservative state legislators and private-sector representatives. They draft and share model legislation for distribution among state governments—on behalf of corporate interests. It has a steely grip (or steal-y grip) on Republicans.

Failures of the Obama Administration to move progressive politics forward dovetails with refusal to release classified documents about the Bay of Pigs (with the claim that the American people couldn't handle such information).

Ted Cruz makes his first appearance.

ELEMENTARY

This is about the militarization of our Public Schools and the proposal of the NRA for armed guards patrolling the schools to keep them "safe." (No need to add commentary on school shootings.)

NSA - IT'S OKAY

The National Security Agency and the troubling future of the surveillance state.

KA-BOOM!

The debate over health care. On one side, moderate Republicans (RINOs), slugging it out with ultra-right "Tea-Baggers" (of the Tea Party Movement) while Karl Rove bashes Ted Cruz. On the other side, Democrat Harry Reid advocating health care based on insurance companies—not single-payer health care. The Public Option got yanked from the table without resistance.

All Hail the Insurance Industry profiting from the suffering of others!

GAS MAN

The horrors of the fracking campaign in Pennsylvania, with imaginary revolts of the plants and animals against the gas man.

STRAIGHT TALK

Spoofing the privatization policies of the Republicans and austerity from hell. These clowns are against anything that would make working-class life better.

Vice President Dick Cheney and others promote torture, whether it works or not. The cruelty is the point!

GAS COMMERICALS

About the gas companies' environmental destruction and dangerous fracking. A company called Range Resources flooded the airwaves. "Range Resources: We're Just Getting Started" (destroying the planet).

PIPELINE

Mayor of Toronto (Whack Job) Rob Ford connects with New Jersey Governor Chris Christie (of Bridge Gate fame), while progressives dream of a more just society and imagine Angelic moves away from the Obama Administration.

HEART ATTACK

Another heart attack brings Dick Cheney back into the limelight. What a Dick!

BULL FIGHT

Corporations and Banks (with their Democratic-Republican pet) entertained by the Koch Brothers egging on a Tea Party bull (that hates the working class). These extreme right-wing views where a precursor to the Trump movement.

There's a subtle shout-out to our old nemesis "Range Resources."

COUPLE OF THE YEAR

Putin and Santorum—a love-match of right-wing figures; with a guest appearance from Henry Kissinger and Fossil Fools. (Remember Allende!)

Supreme Court Justices Roberts, Scalia, and Thomas, and the Citizens United ruling. We're now experiencing the consequences of unlimited corporate cash buying elections.

Also, Dick Cheney's hunting "accident" politicized, and Obama brushing single-payer health care off the table.

This cartoon is about Cliven Bundy's takeover of government land and his stand against the federal government. Donald Sterling was the racist billionaire owner of the LA Clippers who was buying up land and complaining about reverse discrimination. (What a tool!)

On the other side, we see Obama's decision to accept the Keystone XL pipeline.

PITTSBURGH UNDER SIEGE/
WAR MONSTERS

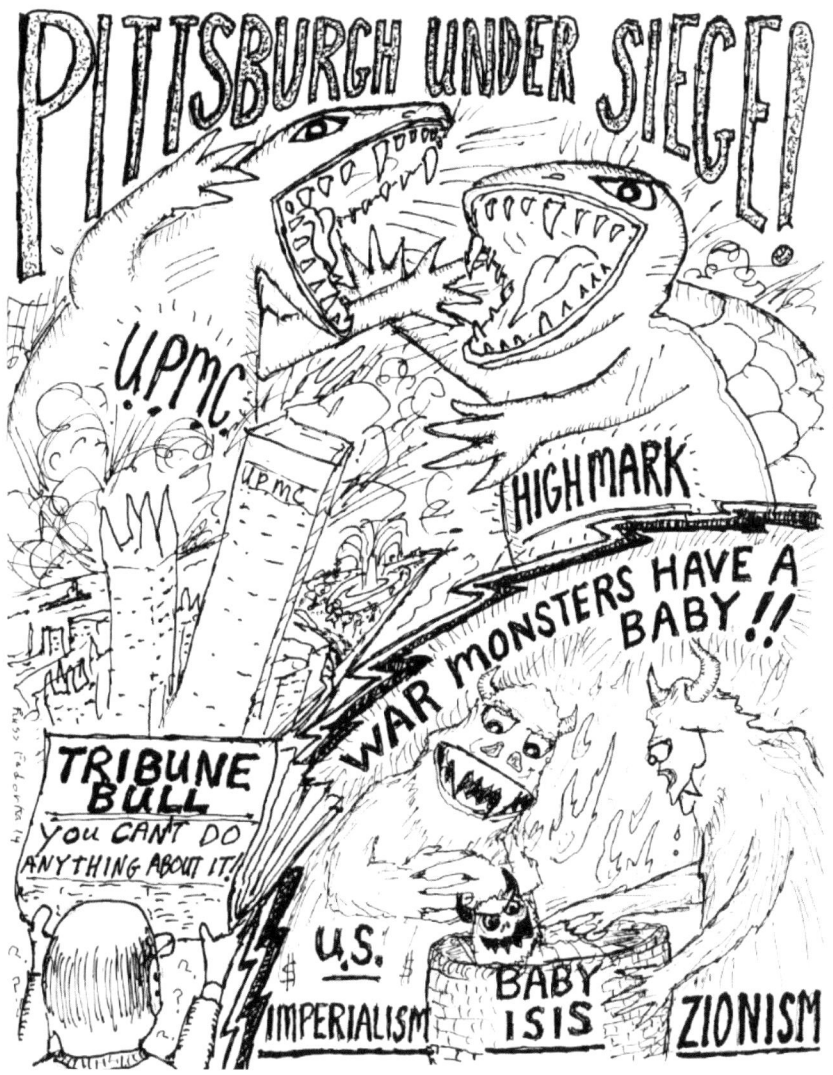

A fierce battle started between two sprawling conglomerates, UPMC and Highmark insurance plans. Choose or die!

    Meanwhile, imperialist interests controlling US foreign policy and militant Zionist interests controlling Israel's domestic and foreign policies, had given birth to the murderous extremism of a new variant of Islamic fundamentalism known as ISIS.

Obama continues Bush-Cheney foreign policies. Meanwhile, Allegheny County Executive Rich Fitzgerald thinks fracking in County Parks is a great idea. It was fiercely opposed by many, including environmentalist Mel Packer (hence the button).

SPACE DISCUSSION

Here's an imaginary take with space aliens looking at the predicament of Earthlings. The bottom half is the former Prime Minister of Iraq, Nouri al-Maliki, and spoofing the CIA.

"Rich the Politician" cashes in with Koch Brothers' money to push for more fracking. Frack You Rich!

BUSH VS. CLINTON?

Dynasties are bad. Early in the Bush versus Clinton campaign, people were thinking that the other Bush brother would be a shoo-in before Trump started his campaign.

Not sure Obama cares too much about pardoning folks busted for weed; he was pretty much "mailing it in" during his last years.

Featuring Harry Reid and John Boehner, the two-party plutocracy overrules "hope and change" every time. And a call to deport White people—starting with Dick Cheney. (With a tip of the cap to Indigenous populations.)

JUST NUTS

Here's a spoof of Trump's Housing Secretary nominee, Dr. Ben Carson. This one got censored because of the Oreo cookie drawn on the side of Carson's head. (It caused a bit of a stir at the time.)

It also calls for ramping up war efforts against Iran.

Obama's endorsement of the trading legislation known as the Trans-Pacific Partnership, and the false Kumbaya moment between the Democrats and Republicans. Mitch McConnell starts to get more airtime.

The barbary of the CIA, how the SOA committed atrocities in Central and South America, and the cover-ups that led to the crisis at the border. Former Texas Governor Rick Perry makes a cameo, as well as a stunning likeness of myself, inviting other cartoonists to jump in on the action.

Inspired by the famous painting, these are the GOP candidates for president loving that corporate cash. What's most notable is the absence of Trump; he wasn't considered a major candidate yet.

MAGIC SANTA

This was a Christmas fantasy of turning weapons into toys. Peace on Earth and good will to all! Welcome to Fantasyland.

HORROR

The horrors of Centrist thinking. There's much talk about left extremism and right extremism, but politically, centralism is the grand enabler of warring barbarity. You also see the imaginary trial of the Bush Administration.

TRICKLE DOWN

The failed policy of the right wing's trickle-down theory and the pushers of Rubio and Cruz at the burial site of Reaganomics.

WALL

The paranoia surrounding the border wall between Mexico and the US and the right-wing fear of birthing aliens to make them legal US citizens. The thought at the time was that Trump was going to be beaten handily by Clinton. (Oops!)

The coat reference was based on a protester getting thrown out of a Trump rally and into the freezing weather without his coat. The cruelty is the point.

Ted Cruz's desire to carpet bomb Iran, and the barbary coming out of both the Trump and Clinton campaigns. Secretary of State Clinton's involvement in Honduras was deplorable. (Get it?!)

Former President, Manuel Zelaya, was unceremoniously shown the door.

ELECTION SANITY

This shows the insanity coming out of candidates Hillary Clinton and Donald Trump as Paul Ryan sells out his last shred of dignity.

REPUBLICANS IMPLODE

The inner squabbling of the Republican Party over the probable nomination of Donald Trump. Future VP Pence is covering for Trump saying he didn't say what he obviously said (and prepping for his 2020 run). Hillary was showing a commanding lead and the feeling was just let Trump talk and he'll put his foot in his mouth. The MSM was more than happy to help. (Double-oops!)

The horror of Trump's victory—who, from this point on, will be known as tRump. Many folks believed he was only running as a publicity stunt.

NUCLEAR WAR

tRump had questioned why we don't use our nukes! This shows VP Pence disabling the button and the ALEC capitalist preparing their legislative agenda. Steve Bannon comes into play for the first time—as a fckn rat.

The infamous PeePee tape was supposed to make a fool of tRump—the golden shower rumor of the time.

The Three Amigos of authoritarianism: the North Korean leader, the US leader, and the Philippines leader; along with tRump's crazy takes on rewriting history.

CIA MCNEWS

The CIA's disinformation campaign, with John Bolton lusting for more war violence. War is great for Wall Street and the MIC!

BAKE SALE

The Pigs of Capitalism trying to bake the Earth and the Resistance trying to stop it. The Big Bad Wolf is on our side this time.

PUERTO RICO

This shows tRump's cruel indifference to the hurricane damage in Puerto Rico and his TV segment showing him tossing paper towels to (or at) the citizens.

TRUMPSANITY

This exposes his insane desire for War and nuclear proliferation. His "alternative facts" are laugh-out-loud whacky.

It's sort of a Dr. Strangelove moment!

WEALTH CAKE

This exposes the fact, at the time, that eight people owned half the wealth of the world. It's a take on trying to feed the other half and the obscene fact that it was true.

TRUMP AND THE LEGION OF DOOM

Fckn Fascists!

TRUMP POURS OVER

This was made during his "combing over" (snark) all the prospects for the Supreme Court. Of course, he ended up with somebody that would do his bidding.

CANNABIS COOKIE

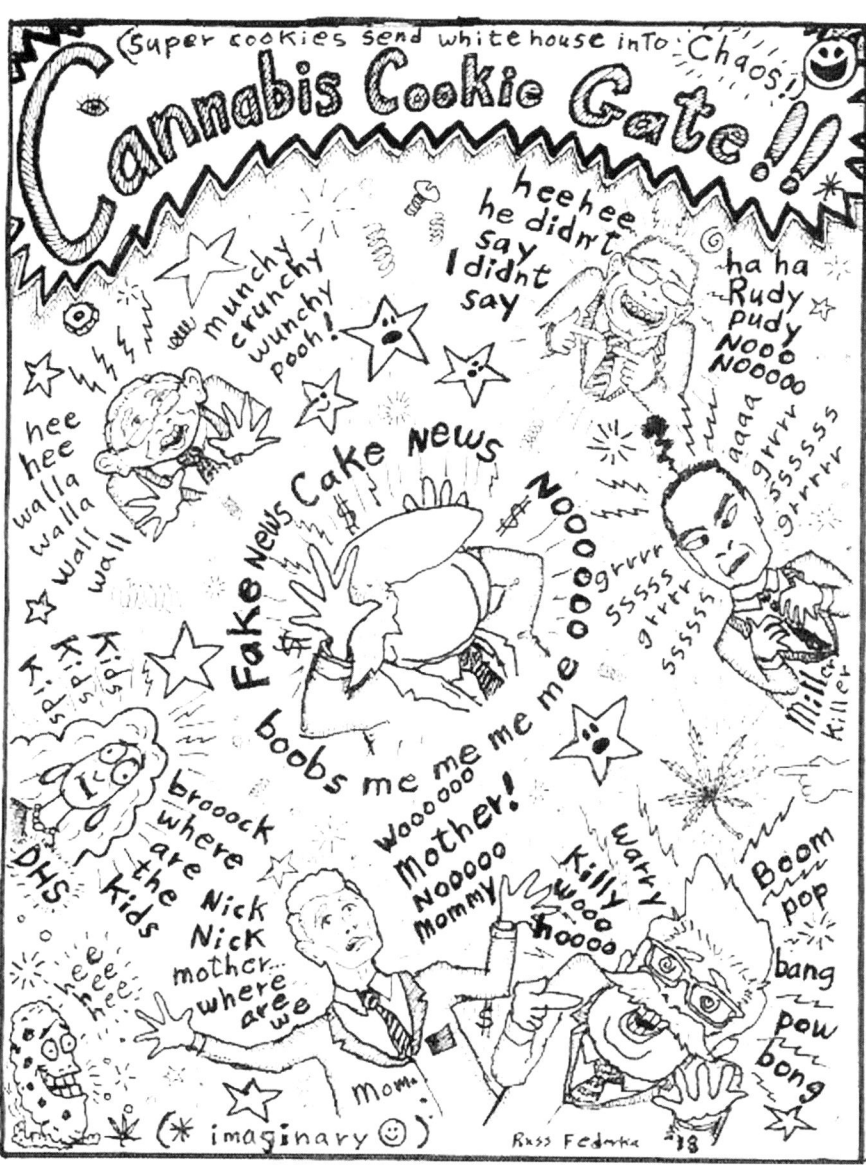

My humorous fantasy of someone delivering cannabis cookies to the White House and how the cast of usual suspects would respond. Characters include Attorney General Jeff Sessions, Rudy Giuliani, Stephen Miller (aka The Antichrist), Warmonger Bolton, VP Pence, and DHS Secretary Kirstjen Nielsen.

ROGERS GETS ROBBED

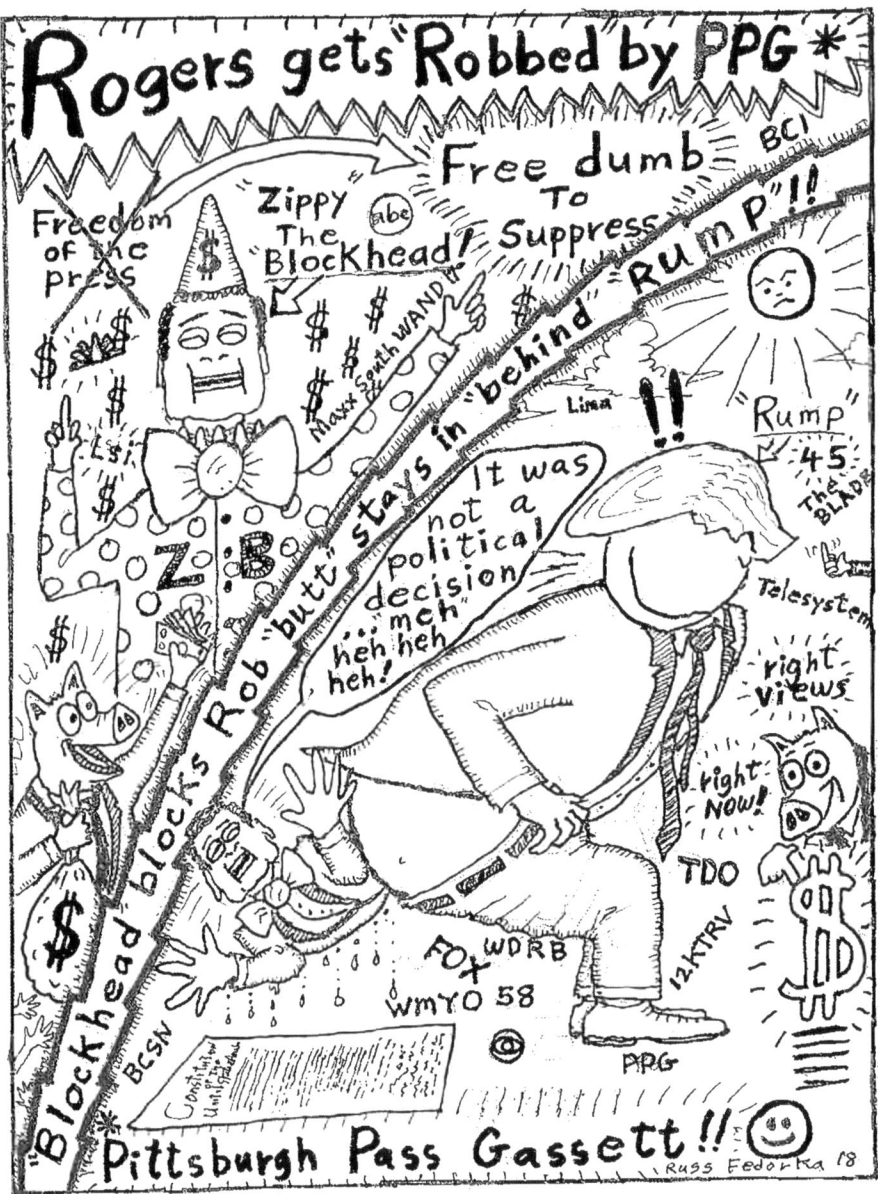

Rob Rogers was the award-winning cartoonist for the Pittsburgh Post-Gazette. His firing was tragic and sent shockwaves through the 'Burgh! The leadership of Mr. Block is contrary to the blue-collar roots of the PG. (With an expression of love for Zippy the Pinhead!)

TRUMP SENDS TROOPS

Taking on all the right-wing loonies jumping up and down about the Border crisis when the actual roots of the problem are borne out by the CIA. Training mercenaries at the School of the Americas has created the hell that continues in Central and South America.

DEMOKINS

This is about the collusion between the Republicans and Democrats in the service of the elites, and how they attack Social Security and empower the Military Industrial Complex together. It also alludes to their attack on Medicare and the fact they both have the same people funding their campaigns!

WE WON

The extreme absurdity of nuclear war and the notion that it could be won. It looks like only the radioactive chickens and the roaches survived (and we're not sure about the chickens).

TRUMP'S MIC PARADE

Remember when Trump was pushing the military parade idea? This is a spoof on how it would look complete with a different kind of pink hat popularized by the women's movement. (Purple-helmeted warriors of love.)

tRump's bragging of how this was the best of times, when of course it wasn't. The war machine never sleeps and the 1% reaps the benefits.

AYN RAMMM

The free marketeers and people like Ayn Rand, and their philosophy of "greed is good." Nothing could be further from the truth. The short-sightedness of putting profit ahead of people and planet is pushing us toward a dystopian hellscape. #Crapitalism

The fantasy of Jesus bursting in on a Board of Directors meeting and freaking everybody right the heck out. (Note: this one is still hanging on the editor's fridge.)

TWO HEADED

This is tRump's way of saying one thing—but what's going on is something opposite. (And now for something completely different...)

CHICKEN HAWKS

This is about the warmongers entrenched in the tRump Administration and how insane it is to rattle the sabers in a nuclear-weapon-filled world. With guest appearances from Bolton, Pompeo, CIA Director "Bloody Gina" Haspel, and Mitch McConnell (and, well, Satan).

The Troika of Tyranny flying around from the tRump Administration—Pompeo, Bolton, and Elliott Abrams (yea, he looks like a vampire). The terrorism and brutality brought on by these three individuals is barbaric. Socialism or Barbarism!

The insane atmosphere around the first impeachment trial of tRump. How could we ever forget it? There's Bill Barr, Pelosi, Turtle-man Mitch (doubling as Dr. No), Rudy Giuliani, and Robert Mueller. What a circus!

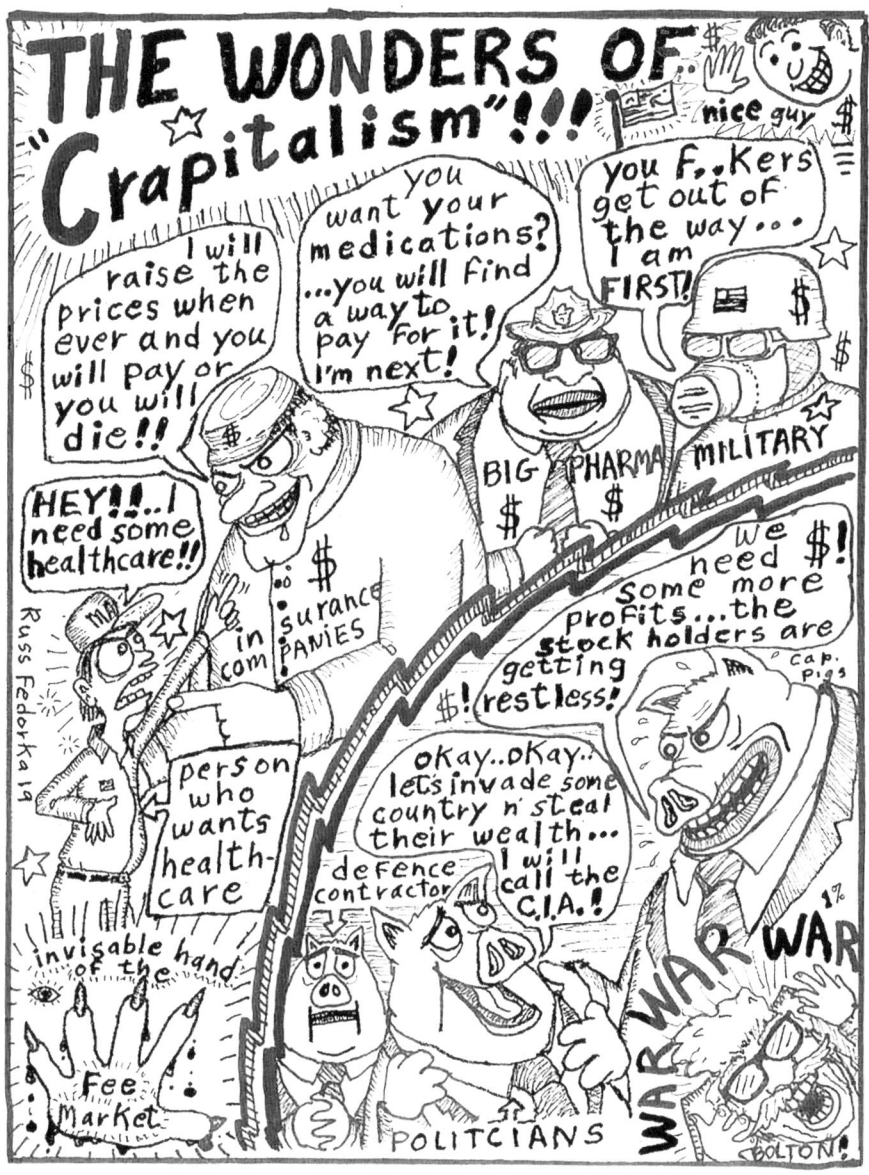

The wonders and brutality of capitalism (aka crapitalism). It exposes the "Lust for Profit" above and beyond all other concerns. One might think the system is rigged against the working-class?!

The Law-and-Order issue that was being bantered around by the tRump administration. With the help of Roger Stone, Rudy Giuliani, Bill Barr, and the Turtle-man.

Tax cuts for the rich! And jack-squat for everyone else. Remember the hurricanes in Puerto Rico and Cuba? Here's more on Trump's response of throwing paper towels at the Puerto Rican population. You can't make this stuff up.

HORNIN IN

I give credit to my buddy Bill who passed away more than a decade ago. He coined the phrase hornin' in. A phrase describing capitalists and their greedy ways; it's quite proper for tRump and his cabinet. There's Pompeo, Bolton, and Pence—always ready to dive in.

The six trillion-dollar nest-egg (about $18,000 per person in the US) that was laid away, supposedly for small businesses. What really happened was that the big corporations kissed tRump's butt and got most of the billions and billions of dollars. Friggin' crapitalists!

FUNNY DAZE

This is about class divide. You can see the rich man in the limousine reaching out for the money as ordinary people are barely getting by. (Pardon me, do you have any Grey Poupon?) tRump was also trying to buy Greenland. (No, really—he said that.)

WARNING: EARTH AHEAD

More aliens wondering "What the hell is happening down there?!"
Although, the kid thinks it's going to be the adventure of a lifetime.

The S.S. tRumpy is sinking but he's not going down with the ship. Get ready for the "Big Lie" and 2024.

ANTIWAR CANDIDATE?

Seems like the election went for "anyone but the last guy." The DNC knows who they serve. Gotta love that Corporate Sponsorship (with apologies to NASCAR).